Dairy-Free, Gluten-Free, and Sugar-Free Cookbook for Kids

Simple Yet Highly Delicious and Nutritious Budget-Friendly Recipes for Kids and Everyone Who Is Lactose and Gluten Intolerant

Introduction

In this guidebook, you will find dairy-free, gluten-free, and sugar-free recipes that are easy to make, kid-friendly, healthy, and delicious, all drawn from various cuisines, seafood, and different types of meat.

Brace yourself for a mouthwatering journey in and out of this book.

PS: I'd like your feedback. If you are happy with this book, please leave a review on Amazon.

Please leave a review for this book on Amazon by visiting the page below:

https://amzn.to/2VMR5qr

Table of Content

Introduction _____ 2

Section 1 _____ 10

Breakfast Recipes _____ 10

#1: Gluten and Dairy-free Pancakes _____ 11

#2: Breakfast Egg Wraps _____ 13

#3: Peanut Butter Cookies _____ 15

#4: Allergy-friendly Carrot Cake _____ 17

#5: Apple Muffins _____ 19

#6: Salmon & Lemon Mini Fish Cakes _____ 21

#7: Cauliflower Wings _____ 23

#8: Turkey Sausage Patties _____ 25

#9: Baked Blueberry and Apple Oatmeal _____ 27

#10: Frittata With Butternut Squash, Bacon & Mushroom _____ 29

#11: Oatmeal Cookies with Blueberry & Peach _ 31

#12: Southwest Egg Scramble _____ 33

#13: Chocolate Orange Chia Parfait _____ 35

#14: Berry Peach Smoothie _____ 37

#15: Raw Banana Cashew Yogurt _____ 38

#16: Grain-Free Granola _____ 39

#17: Kiwi Oatmeal Bowl _____ 41

#18: Protein Porridge _____ 43

#19: Mango Oatmeal Bowl _____ 45

#20: Banana Flour Waffles _____ 47

#21: Sweet Potato Waffles _____ 49

#22: Blueberry Banana Muffins _____ 51

Section 2 _____ 53

Lunch Recipes _____ 53

#23: Bean and bangers one-pot _____ 54

#24: Popcorn Chicken _____ 56

#25: Peanut butter chicken _____ 58

#26: Cranberry Tuna Salad on Apple Slices __ 60

#27: Smoked Salmon Salad in Avocado Boats__ 61

#28: Sweet Potato Fries 63

#29: Zoodles With Garlicky Shrimp 65

#30: Minty Pea & Potato Soup 67

#31: Coconut Chicken Curry with Potatoes ___ 69

#32: Baked Coconut & Chicken Tenders 71

#33: Broccoli Fritters 73

#34: Skillet Cod with Fresh Tomatoes & Basil _ 75

#35: Instant Pot Kale, Squash, and Chicken Soup 77

#36: Turkey Cranberry Meatballs with Cranberry Orange Sauce 79

#37: Salmon Balls 82

#38: Cajun Sweet Potato Fries 84

#39: Slow Cooker Curry Chicken Legs 86

#40: Sheet Pan Roasted Brussel sprouts, Butternut, and Bacon 88

#41: Pan-seared Duck Breast with Cranberry Maple Syrup 90

#42: Oven Roasted Brussels Sprouts with Bacon 92

#43: Strawberry Mango Spinach Salad 94

#44: Gluten-Free Chicken Nuggets 96

Ingredients 96

#45: Ground Beef with Kale and Mushrooms 98

#46: Quiche with Easy Quinoa Crust 100

#47: Garlic Balsamic Roasted Potatoes and Asparagus 102

#48: Thai Basil Chicken Stir Fry 104

Section 3 106

Dinner Recipes 106

#49: Butter bean, chorizo & spinach baked eggs 107

#50: Oven-baked Thai Chicken Rice 109

#51: Salmon and Avocado Salsa 111

#52: Broccoli & Beef Teriyaki Noodle Bowls 113

#53: Lemon Chicken and Asparagus Sheet Pan Dinner _____ 115

#54: Foil Packet Grilled Mahi Mahi _____ 117

#55: Roasted Cauliflower & Garlic Soup _____ 119

#56: Instant Pot Ribs _____ 121

#57: Guacamole Stuffed Chicken Breast _____ 123

#58: Ground Turkey Brussels Sprouts Skillet _____ 126

#59: Spicy Shrimp and Brussels Sprout Stir-Fry _____ 128

#60: Ground Beef Curry _____ 130

#61: Maple Mustard Chicken with Fall Vegetables _____ 132

#62: Instant Pot Spicy Orange Beef _____ 134

#63: Turkey Sweet Potato Skillet _____ 137

#64: Red Rice with Sausage and Peppers _____ 139

#65: Red Curry Chicken Wings _____ 141

#66: Instant Pot Venison Roast _____ 143

#67: Baked Chicken Thighs _____ 146

#68: Quinoa Stuffed Chicken _____ 148

#69: Keto coconut curry chicken _____ 151

#70: Shrimp and Scallion Stir-Fry _____ 153

#71: Easy Jambalaya _____ 155

#72: Salmon with olive-pistachio tapenade and tomatoes _____ 158

#73: Kielbasa and Lentil Rice with Spinach __ 160

#74: Prosciutto-Wrapped Salmon Skewers __ 162

Conclusion _____ 164

Section 1
Breakfast Recipes

#1: Gluten and Dairy-free Pancakes

Serves: 4

Cook time:20 minutes

Ingredients

Coconut oil

1 teaspoon of vanilla extract

2 tablespoons of chia seeds

1 egg

1 banana

1 ½ cups of almond milk

1 cup of buckwheat flour

Instructions

Add all the ingredients in a food processor apart from the coconut oil and process into a smooth batter.

Melt a teaspoon of coconut oil in a medium/hot pan and swirl the oil in the pan.

Pour the batter into the hot pan, forming a pancake.

Flip over each pancake as soon as bubbles appear on the batter and cook the other side.

Cook all the pancakes until there is no batter left.

Serve with maple syrup and berries.

#2: Breakfast Egg Wraps

Serves: 4

Cook time: 12 minutes

Ingredients

4 teaspoons of gluten-free English mustard powder made up with water

10 eggs

8 tablespoons of gluten-free porridge oats

2 generous handfuls of finely chopped parsley

8 tomatoes cut into wedges

4 teaspoons of cold-pressed rapeseed oil, and 2 extra drops

250g of closed cup mushrooms

Instructions

Slice the mushrooms into thick pieces.

Add 2 teaspoons of rapeseed oil in a nonstick pan and heat. Once the oil is heated, add the mushrooms, give them a good stir, then place the lid on and fry for 6-8 minutes.

Add in half of the tomatoes and stir; cook with the lid off for 1-2 minutes until the tomatoes soften.

Whisk the eggs and parsley until well mixed.

Place a large nonstick frying pan on the heat and heat a drop of oil.

Pour a quarter of the egg mixture into the pan and fry until the egg is almost set —about a minute should do it—then flip over.

Tip the egg from the pan and spread ¼ of the mustard, scoop a quarter of the filling down to the center, then roll it up.

Fry the rest of the egg mix until there is none left.

#3: Peanut Butter Cookies

Serves: 12

Cook time: 25 minutes

Ingredients

1 teaspoon of sugar-free vanilla extract

1 egg

½ cup of stevia

1 cup of peanut butter

Instructions

Preheat the oven to 175 degrees C and line a baking sheet with parchment paper.

Whisk the peanut butter, sweetener, egg, and vanilla extract in a bowl until a dough forms.

Roll out the dough into 1-inch balls.

Transfer the balls on the prepared sheet and press down using a fork, making a crisscross pattern.

Place in the oven and bake for 12 to 15 minutes until the edges are golden.

Allow the cookies to cool on the baking sheet.

Transfer them to a wire rack to completely cool.

#4: Allergy-friendly Carrot Cake

Serves: 10

Cook time: 50 minutes

Ingredients

1 tablespoon of lemon juice

1 teaspoon of baking soda

¼ teaspoon of sea salt

¼g of nutmeg

½ teaspoon of ground ginger

½ teaspoon of ground cinnamon

½ cup of coconut milk

½ cup of melted coconut milk

1 cup of Teff flour

2 cups of carrots, peeled and chopped

¼ cup of boiling water

¼ cup of sultanas

6 pitted Medjool dates

Instructions

Preheat the oven to 165 degrees C fan-forced.

Grease a 12-hole muffin tin and put it aside.

Place the dates and raisins in a small heatproof bowl, pour the ½ cup of boiling water, replace the lid and let it sit for 20 minutes.

Add the carrots to a blender and pulse 10 times into smaller pieces.

Transfer the soaked raisins and dates with the water into the blender, add the teff flour, melted coconut oil, coconut milk, the spices, and pulse 8-10 times until well mixed.

Add in the salt, baking soda, lemon juice, and pulse 2-3 times.

Pour the mixture into the greased muffin tin, each hole ¾ full, and place in the oven for 35-40 minutes.

Insert a toothpick at the center of the cake, and if it comes out clean, the cake is ready.

Serve topped with whipped coconut cream if desired.

#5: Apple Muffins

Serves: 12 muffins

Cook time: 30 minutes

Ingredients

1 large apple, peeled and sliced

1 teaspoon of cinnamon

1 teaspoon of sugar-free vanilla extract

¼ teaspoon of baking soda

2 large eggs

¼ cup of chestnut flour

1 cup of almond flour

¼ cup of organic unsweetened apple sauce

¼ coconut oil

Instructions

Preheat oven to 170 degrees C.

Add all the ingredients to a blender or food processor, and mix, whisk in the diced apple.

Line the baking tray with muffin cups and scoop the mixture into them.

Bake in the preheated oven until the tops start browning — about 20 minutes.

Cool the muffins before eating.

#6: Salmon & Lemon Mini Fish Cakes

Serves: Makes 20 cakes

Cook time: 45 minutes

Ingredients

Enough oil for frying

2 tablespoons of gluten-free flour mixed with a teaspoon of coarsely ground pepper

1 tablespoon of parsley, chopped, plus more

140g of smoked salmon trimmings, plus more to serve

1 egg yolk

Grated lemon zest

Juice of ½ lemon

2 tablespoons of olive oil

2 large potatoes for baking

Instructions

Put the potatoes in the microwave for 10 minutes on high until tender and allow them to cool for 5 minutes.

Spoon the potatoes flesh in a bowl, mash, and allow them to cool.

Add the olive oil, lemon zest, and lemon juice enough to taste, then whisk in the egg, salmon, and parsley until well mixed.

Cut into small 3cm wide and 1cm deep rounds, then chill in the fridge for 15 minutes.

Coat the fish cakes with the peppered flour and use a little oil to fry over low heat for 2-3 minutes per side.

Drain on paper towels.

To serve garnish with salmon and parsley.

#7: Cauliflower Wings

Serves: 4

Cook time: 35 minutes

Ingredients

2 tablespoons of nutritional yeast

1 teaspoon curry powder

1 teaspoon onion powder

¾ cup of chickpea flour

1 cup plus 2 tablespoons of unsweetened, plain almond milk

¾ bottle of Wing-Time Buffalo Sauce

1 large head of cauliflower

Instructions

Preheat oven to 450 degrees F.

Lightly spray a large nonstick baking sheet with oil.

Cut the cauliflower into florets.

Mix the flour, spices, and the nutritional yeast into a bowl and whisk until well mixed.

Toss a handful of cauliflower pieces in almond milk and then into the flour mixture.

Transfer onto the prepared baking sheet and bake in the oven for 20 minutes until crispy.

Place a medium-sized saucepan over medium-low heat and heat the Wing-Time sauce.

Stir in 2 tablespoons of almond milk into the pan.

Turn the cauliflower using a wooden spoon and broil it for 5-7 minutes, with the oven open, until it turns brown.

Transfer the now cooked cauliflower into a large bowl, pour the hot sauce over the cauliflower, then toss to coat.

Serve with a dipping of choice if desired.

#8: Turkey Sausage Patties

Serves: 36 patties

Cook time: 30 minutes

Ingredients

1 tablespoon of pure maple syrup

1 teaspoon of salt

1 teaspoon of garlic powder

1 tablespoon of onion powder

1 tablespoon of dried sage

1 tablespoon of dried thyme

3 lbs. of ground turkey

Instructions

Mix all the seasonings in a large bowl.

Add in the maple syrup and whisk until well combined.

Add the turkey to the bowl and, using your hands, mix thoroughly.

Place a skillet over medium-high heat and spray with nonstick cooking spray.

Make patties from the turkey sausage, and fry in the skillet until both sides are brown and the center is not pink but cooked.

Serve warm!

#9: Baked Blueberry and Apple Oatmeal

Serves: 4

Cook time: 55 minutes

Ingredients

1 cup of fresh blueberries, divided

2 small apples, peeled and chopped

1 teaspoon of sugar-free vanilla extract

1½ tablespoons of non-dairy butter, melted and slightly cooled

1 large egg

3 tablespoons of pure maple syrup

1 cup milk of choice

¼ teaspoon of fine sea salt

¾ teaspoon of ground cinnamon

½ teaspoon of baking powder

½ cup of raw walnuts or pecans, chopped and divided

1 cup old-fashioned rolled oats

Instructions

Preheat your oven to 375 degrees F, grease a 2-quart baking dish with olive oil spray, and put it aside.

Combine the oats, half of the nuts, baking powder, cinnamon, and salt in a medium-sized bowl.

Whip together the milk, maple syrup, egg, butter, and vanilla in a different medium-sized bowl.

Sprinkle the apples evenly at the bottom of the greased baking, cover them with half of the blueberries, top with the oat mixture, and pour the liquid mixture evenly.

Sprinkle the rest of the nuts and blueberries, then bake until the oats have set — about 35 to 40 minutes.

Let it sit for 5 minutes before serving.

#10: Frittata With Butternut Squash, Bacon & Mushroom

Serves: 6

Cook time: 1 hour 15 minutes

Ingredients

¼ teaspoon of sea salt

1/3 cup of fresh oregano, chopped

12 eggs, beaten

4 cups of baby spinach

2 cups of mushrooms, sliced

2 cups of butternut squash, peeled and chopped

4 slices of thick-cut bacon

Instructions

Preheat the oven to 350 degrees F.

Place a skillet over medium heat and cook the bacon for 2 minutes on each side.

Place the ready bacon on a chopping board, and once cool, chop the bacon and put it aside.

Add the butternut to the skillet, and cook covered over medium heat for about 5 minutes until the squash starts softening.

Add the mushrooms and cook until they begin to turn brown and soft —for about 5 minutes.

Add the spinach, oregano, salt and cook covered until the spinach wilts —for about 2 minutes. Add the chopped bacon, then set the skillet off the heat.

Pour the beaten eggs into the mixture, and using a wooden spoon, gently start mixing well with the vegetables, making sure you have an even distribution.

Transfer the skillet into the preheated oven and bake for 35-40 minutes until the frittata has cooked through and is golden brown.

Allow the frittata to sit for 10 minutes before serving.

#11: Oatmeal Cookies with Blueberry & Peach

Serves:14 cookies

Cook time: 55 minutes

Ingredients

¼ cup of maple syrup crystals for sprinkling

½ teaspoon of baking powder+ ½ teaspoon of lemon juice

1/8 teaspoon of salt

A pinch of stevia extract powder

½ cup of fresh wild blueberries

1 large fresh peach, cubed

1/3 cup of grapeseed oil

1/3 cup of golden flaxseeds, freshly ground

¾ cup of almond flour or any seed flour of choice

1 cup of sugar-free apple sauce

2 cups of organic, gluten-free rolled oats

Instructions

Preheat oven to 360 degrees F, then line a baking sheet with parchment paper.

Whip the apple sauce, oil, and flaxseeds together in a bowl.

Mix the oats, flour, baking soda + lemon juice, salt, and stevia extract in another bowl.

Pour the apple sauce mixture into the bowl with the flour mixture and mix until well combined.

Scoop the cookie dough with a spoon or spatula into 14 rounded scoops onto the prepared baking sheet and place the peach chunks and blueberries on top.

Sprinkle the maple syrup crystals on top.

Place in the oven for 35-40 minutes. Once done, allow to cool on the sheet before transferring to a cooling rack.

#12: Southwest Egg Scramble

Serves: 3

Cook time: 20 minutes

Ingredients

Chopped cilantro for garnish

¼ teaspoon of cayenne pepper

½ teaspoon of salt

½ teaspoon of smoked paprika

½ teaspoon of cumin

1 medium ear corn, kernels removed

1 medium jalapeno, seeded and minced

1 small red bell pepper, chopped

½ red onion, chopped

1½ tablespoons of olive oil

6 large eggs

Instructions

Whisk the eggs in a medium bowl and set them aside.

Heat a large nonstick skillet over medium heat, then add the oil, and once hot, add in the onion and fry for 2 minutes.

Add the pepper, jalapeno, corn, cumin, paprika, salt, and cayenne and cook until the pepper is crispy tender —for about 3-5 minutes— then transfer the vegetables to a bowl.

Lower the heat slightly, pour the eggs into the now-empty skillet, and cook, occasionally stirring until the eggs are scrambled, then set away from heat.

Add the vegetables into the skillet, and garnish with cilantro.

Serve as desired!

#13: Chocolate Orange Chia Parfait

Serves: 2

Cook time: 5 minutes

Ingredients

½ teaspoon of cinnamon

Zest of an orange

¼ cup of soft dates, pitted

3 tablespoons of cacao

3 tablespoons of chia

1 cup of non-dairy milk of choice

To serve:

1 orange, peeled and blended

½ cup of pomegranate seeds

Instructions

Mix the milk and chia in a container and refrigerate overnight or until the pudding has set.

Add the chia pudding, cacao, dates, orange zest, and cinnamon in a food processor or blender and blend until smooth.

Chill in the refrigerator for 30 minutes.

Place ¼ cup of pomegranate seeds at the bottom of the jar, followed by ½ cup of the pudding, topping with half the orange sauce.

Do the same with another jar until you are out of ingredients.

Enjoy when cold.

#14: Berry Peach Smoothie

Serves: 1

Cook time: 12 minutes

Ingredients

½ cup of pomegranate juice, fresh

1 tablespoon of golden organic flaxseeds

2 stalks of celery

1 cup of carrot greens

½ cup of frozen strawberries

½ cup of frozen wild blueberries

½ cup of frozen sliced peaches

Instructions

Add all the ingredients to a blender and blend to desired smoothness.

Serve immediately.

#15: Raw Banana Cashew Yogurt

Serves: 2

Cook time: 5 minutes

Ingredients

½ teaspoon of dairy-free probiotic powder

A pinch of sea salt

2/3 cup of coconut water

1½ tablespoons of freshly squeezed lemon juice

2 large bananas

1 cup of cashews, soaked for 2 hours, then drained

Instructions

Add all the ingredients to a blender until smooth.

Serve topped with whole cashews if desired.

#16: Grain-Free Granola

Serves: 4

Cook time: 35 minutes

Ingredients

60 grams of dried cranberries

¼ cup of melted coconut oil

¼ cup of maple syrup

½ teaspoon of sea salt

1 teaspoon of cinnamon

¼ cup of chia seeds

1 cup of unsweetened shredded coconut

1 cup of pumpkin seeds

1 cup of sunflower seeds

Instructions

Preheat the oven to 150 degrees C. Line a large baking sheet with parchment paper and put it aside.

Mix the salt, cinnamon, chia, coconut, pumpkin seeds, and sunflower seeds in a large bowl until they are combined well.

Pour the maple syrup as well as the melted coconut into the bowl and mix well using a wooden spoon.

Transfer the granola to your prepared sheet, spread evenly, and bake in the oven for 30-35 minutes.

Allow the granola to cool completely, then break into pieces before adding the dried cranberries.

Enjoy!

#17: Kiwi Oatmeal Bowl

Serves: 2

Cook time: 25 minutes

Ingredients

1 tablespoon of maple syrup

7 almonds, chopped

1 tablespoon of sunflower and pumpkin seeds mix

¼ cup of hemp milk

1 handful of greens

½ avocado

1 large kiwi, sliced

½ cup of organic, gluten-free cooked rolled oats

Instructions

Add ½ cup of rolled oats, a cup of water, and salt to taste in a small skillet, and bring to a boil. Turn off the heat and allow the oats to sit covered for 10 minutes until all the water is absorbed.

Add all the other ingredients to a blender and blend.

Spoon the oatmeal in a bowl, pour the green smoothie over the oats, sprinkle the almonds, sunflower, and pumpkin seeds, and top with a drizzle of the maple syrup.

Voila!

#18: Protein Porridge

Serves: 3-4

Cook time:

Ingredients

¼ cup of unsweetened shredded coconut

¼ cup of freshly ground flaxseeds

¼ cup of hemp seeds

¼ teaspoon of ground cardamom

¼ teaspoon of ground cloves

½ teaspoon of ground cinnamon

1 vanilla pod, split open with seeds scraped

2 cups of non-dairy milk

Instructions

Pour the non-dairy milk and the vanilla pod contents into a small pot and bring to a simmer.

Add in the cinnamon, cloves, and the cardamom and stir until mixed, then add the hemp, flax, and the coconut and cook over low heat, allowing the mixture to thicken.

Let it cool, then serve topped with blueberries, walnuts, and maple syrup if desired.

#19: Mango Oatmeal Bowl

Serves: 2

Cook time: 25 minutes

Ingredients

½ teaspoon of chia

1 tablespoon of pumpkin and sunflower seed mix, raw

1/3 cup of frozen plant milk

1 tablespoon of flax seeds

½ banana

1 fresh mango, cubed

½ cup of organic, gluten-free rolled oats, cooked

Instructions

Place ½ cup of rolled oats and a cup of water in a skillet and bring to boil.

Remove from heat and allow to sit covered for 10 minutes for water absorption.

Add the rest of the ingredients to a blender and blend to make a smoothie.

Spoon the oatmeal in a bowl, pour the smoothie over, and sprinkle on your desired toppings.

#20: Banana Flour Waffles

Serves: 6

Cook time: 20 minutes

Ingredients

¾ cup of almond milk

2 tablespoons of oil

2 eggs

A pinch of salt

1 teaspoon of baking powder

1/3 cup of almond flour

1 cup of banana flour

Instructions

Preheat your waffle maker.

Add all the dry ingredients to a large bowl and mix until well combined.

Pour in the wet ingredients into the bowl and whisk until blended.

Add the waffle batter into the waffler iron and cover the lid.

Cook for 3-5 minutes, and once ready, remove the waffle using a fork.

Make the rest of the waffles until there is no batter left.

Serve the waffles with pecans and maple syrup if desired.

#21: Sweet Potato Waffles

Serves: 2

Cook time: 15 minutes

Ingredients

1/3 cup of unsweetened almond milk

½ tablespoon of coconut oil

2 tablespoons of maple syrup

1½ teaspoons of vanilla

2 eggs

¾ cup peeled, cooked, and mashed sweet potato

½ teaspoon of nutmeg

1 teaspoon of cinnamon

½ teaspoon of salt

½ teaspoon of baking soda

2 tablespoons of coconut flour

1 cup of almond flour

Instructions

Preheat the waffle iron.

Whisk all the dry ingredients in a large bowl.

Whip all the wet ingredients in a different bowl.

Pour the wet ingredients into the dry ingredients and mix until well blended.

Pour the batter into the waffle iron and use a spatula to spread it.

Cook the rest of the waffles until none is left.

Serve with desired toppings.

#22: Blueberry Banana Muffins

Serves: 12 muffins

Cook time: 20 minutes

Ingredients

1 cup of fresh blueberries

1 teaspoon of pure vanilla extract

2 large eggs, beaten

1 teaspoon of lemon zest

½ teaspoon of cinnamon

½ cup of pure maple syrup

A pinch of salt

¼ teaspoon of xanthan gum

1½ cups of any gluten-free flour

1 teaspoon of baking soda

1/3 cup of melted coconut oil

3 very ripe bananas, mashed

Instructions

Preheat the oven to 350 degrees F.

Spray your muffin tin with some cooking spray —you can also use baking cup liners.

Mash the bananas with a fork in a bowl until completely smooth.

Add the baking soda in the bowl with bananas and mix until combined; allow the mixture to stand for 1-2 minutes.

Whisk in the melted coconut oil into the bowl with the mashed bananas.

Add the vanilla extract, the beaten eggs, salt and the maple syrup and then stir until combined.

Add in the xantham gum, dried lemon peel, cinnamon and the gluten-free flour.

Stir in the blueberries gently.

Scoop the batter into the prepared muffin tray and bake in the oven for 15-20 minutes.

Let the muffins cool and enjoy.

Section 2

Lunch Recipes

#23: Bean and bangers one-pot

Serves: 4

Cook time: 40 minutes

Ingredients

2 tablespoons of gluten-free Dijon mustard

100g of frozen peas

400ml of chicken stock

2 cans of gluten-free mixed beans in water, 410g each, drained and rinsed

2 tablespoons of red wine vinegar

2 onions, halved lengthways, and sliced

8 good-quality gluten-free sausages

1 tablespoon of olive oil

Instructions

Pour the oil into a large pan, heat the oil, then sizzle the sausages, occasionally turning —cook for 6 minutes until all sides are brown— then transfer onto a plate.

Add the carrots and onions into the pan and cook, occasionally stirring —for 8 minutes until the onions are tender.

Pour the vinegar into the pan and mix in the drained beans.

Stream in the stock, add the sausages with the beans and bring to simmer for 10 minutes.

Spread in the frozen peas, cooking for 2 minutes until the peas have heated through, then turn off the heat.

Whip in the mustard and adjust the seasoning and serve.

#24: Popcorn Chicken

Serves: 4

Cook time: 25 minutes

Ingredients

Coconut oil

2 large eggs

Salt to taste

1 teaspoon of garlic powder

1 cup of gluten-free oats

2 large chicken breasts

Instructions

Process the oats in a food processor into coarse flour.

Mix the garlic powder, salt and ground oats in a shallow bowl, and put it aside.

Whisk the eggs in another bowl.

Chop the chicken breasts into bite-sized pieces.

Dip the chicken pieces into the egg mixture, then pass through the oat mixture until coated.

Heat the coconut oil in a large frying pan and shallow fry the chicken until it cooks through for 4 minutes on each side and season with salt

Serve with desired dipping sauce.

#25: Peanut butter chicken

Serves: 4

Cook time: 50 minutes

Ingredients

400g chopped tomatoes

1 bunch of coriander, ½ roughly chopped and ½ leaves picked

400ml coconut milk

100g smooth peanut butter

2 teaspoons of garam masala

2 teaspoons of freshly grated ginger

2 red chilies, deseeded

1 garlic clove, crushed

8 skinless, boneless chicken thighs, cut into chunks

2 tablespoons of vegetable oil

Instructions

Place a deep-frying pan over medium heat and heat a tablespoon of oil.

Fry the chicken chunks in batches until golden brown and set aside.

Add another tablespoon of oil into the pan and fry the garlic, chili, and ginger for 1 minute.

Add in the garam masala and fry for another minute.

Mix in the peanut butter, coconut milk, and tomatoes and bring to simmer.

Transfer the chicken into the pan, add the chopped coriander and cook until the sauce thickens and the chicken cooks through —for 30 minutes.

Serve garnished with the rest of the coriander, roasted peanuts, and rice if desired.

#26: Cranberry Tuna Salad on Apple Slices

Serves: 4

Cook time: 10 minutes

Ingredients

4 medium sweet apples

8 tablespoons of cranberries

4 cans of tuna packed in water, well-drained

Salt and pepper to taste

4 teaspoons of apple cider vinegar

4 tablespoons of gluten-free mayonnaise

Instructions

Add the mayo, vinegar, salt, pepper to a bowl and whisk until smooth.

Add in the tuna and cranberries and whip until combined.

Slice the apples into rounds, making sturdy apple slices.

Scoop the salad on the apple slices.

#27: Smoked Salmon Salad in Avocado Boats

Serves: 2-4

Cook time: 10 minutes

Ingredients

2 ripe avocados, halved, pitted, and scooped out of the peel with a big spoon

Salt to taste

3 tablespoons of finely chopped green onions

½ pound of smoked salmon, chopped

2 grinds fresh pepper

1½ teaspoons of lemon juice, plus more for spritzing

3 tablespoons of gluten-free mayonnaise

Instructions

Add the mayo, lemon juice, and pepper to a medium bowl and mix until combined.

Add the smoked salmon and the green onions and toss to combine, then taste and adjust seasoning.

Chill the salad for a few hours to enhance flavor —this step is optional.

Salt the avocado halves and spritz with some lemon juice.

Spoon the salad into the avocado halves and serve immediately.

#28: Sweet Potato Fries

Serves: 4-6

Cook time: 60 minutes

Ingredients

1 tablespoon of lemon juice

1 garlic clove, minced

¾ cup of gluten-free mayonnaise

½ teaspoon of freshly ground black pepper

2 teaspoons of salt

2 tablespoons of fresh basil, chopped

3 tablespoons of olive oil

5 sweet potatoes, cut into 1 *5- inch fries

Instructions

Preheat oven to 400 degrees F.

Line a baking sheet with foil and place on the fries, tossing with olive oil.

Next, bake in the oven for 45 minutes until golden.

Mix the basil, salt, and pepper in a small bowl, and in a different bowl, whisk the mayonnaise, garlic, and lemon juice until combined.

Sprinkle the basil salt on the now-ready fries.

Serve with the garlic mayonnaise as a dip.

#29: Zoodles With Garlicky Shrimp

Serves: 4

Cook time: 15 minutes

Ingredients

1 teaspoon of lemon zest

1 tablespoon of lemon juice

6 cups of zucchini noodles

1/8 teaspoon of ground black pepper

½ teaspoon of salt

6 garlic cloves, minced

1 pound of jumbo shrimp, shelled and deveined

2 tablespoons of olive oil

Instructions

Place a large skillet over medium heat, add olive oil, and heat for about 2 minutes.

Stir in the shrimp, garlic, salt, and pepper, allowing the shrimp to cook on one side for 3 minutes.

Stir and flip over the shrimp, making sure the garlic does not burn, then cook the other side for 1-2 minutes.

Transfer the shrimp into a bowl using a slotted spoon and put it aside.

Add the zoodles into the skillet and cook for 3 minutes, stirring often.

Finally, add the lemon zest and juice as well as the cooked shrimp then continue stirring, and cook for 2 more minutes.

Serve immediately!

#30: Minty Pea & Potato Soup

Serves: 4

Cook time: 30 minutes

Ingredients

A handful of mint, chopped

350g of frozen peas

Vegetable stock

800g of potatoes, peeled and cut into small chunks

1 onion, chopped

2 teaspoons of vegetable oil

Instructions

Heat oil in a large saucepan and fry the onions until softened—for 5 minutes.

Add in the potatoes and the stock and bring to a boil.

Simmer covered for 10 to 15 minutes. Add the peas 2 minutes towards the end.

Remove ¼ of the vegetables using a slotted spoon and put them aside.

Blend the rest of the vegetables using a hand blender until smooth.

Stir in the reserved vegetables, the chopped mint, and adjust seasoning.

Serve with gluten-free bread if desired.

#31: Coconut Chicken Curry with Potatoes

Serves: 4

Cook time: 25 minutes

Ingredients

4 tablespoons of coconut oil

Salt to taste

4 tablespoons of a mixture of curry paste and curry powder

13.5 oz of full-fat coconut milk

5 cloves of garlic, minced

1 russet potato, cut into 1-inch cubes

1 onion, sliced

1lb of boneless skinless chicken thighs, cut into 1-inch pieces

Instructions

Peel and cut the potatoes into small cubes, chop the onions and garlic, and cut the chicken into small cubes.

Heat a large skillet and melt 2 tablespoons of coconut oil; add the curry powder and paste, swirling it until blended.

Pour in the coconut milk and stir until well mixed.

Add the potatoes to the curry, bring to a boil and then allow it to simmer.

Place a different skillet on heat, melt 2 tablespoons of coconut oil, then fry the garlic and onions for a minute, stirring to ensure the garlic does not burn.

Add the chicken cubes and cook, stirring for 5 minutes, then turn off the heat.

Transfer the chicken into the skillet with the coconut curry and allow it to cook for 10 minutes.

Serve with your desired accompaniment and enjoy!

#32: Baked Coconut & Chicken Tenders

Serves: 4

Cook time: 23 minutes

Ingredients

Cooking Spray

8 chicken tenders

¾ cup of shredded sweetened coconut

¾ cup gluten-free panko bread crumbs

Salt and pepper to taste

2 teaspoons of garlic powder

2 large eggs

Instructions

Preheat the oven to 400 degrees F. Prepare a large baking sheet by spraying with cooking spray.

Whip the eggs, garlic powder, salt, and pepper in a wide shallow dish until well blended.

Add the bread crumbs and shredded coconut into another shallow dish and mix until well combined.

Dip the chicken in the egg mixture, coat both sides with the mixture, lift the chicken, allowing the excess egg mixture to drip off.

Pass the moist chicken into the coconut mixture, completely coating the chicken, then transfer onto the prepared baking sheet.

Scrap the excess egg as well as the coconut mixture after preparing all the chicken pieces.

Spray your chicken tenders with some cooking spray, just the tops, and place on the oven rack in the middle.

Bake until the chicken cooks through and the coating turns crisp and golden, —for 12-14 minutes.

Allow the chicken to cool before serving.

#33: Broccoli Fritters

Serves: Makes 8 fritters

Cook time: 25 minutes

Ingredients

2 tablespoons of olive oil

2 cloves of garlic, minced

1 teaspoon of gluten-free Dijon mustard

¼ cup of nutritional Gluten-free yeast

2 eggs

¾ cups of almond flour

½ cups of chopped steamed broccoli

Instructions

Cut the steamed broccoli florets into small pieces and slice the stalks into small thin slices.

Process the almond flour, eggs, nutritional yeast, Dijon mustard, and garlic in a food processor until well blended.

Add the chopped broccoli and mix well.

Place a frying pan over medium heat and add the olive oil.

Scoop the batter and form small patties in the pan and cook them for 3 minutes.

Flip the fritters once they are lightly golden brown and fry the other side for 2-3 minutes.

Transfer the fritters to a paper towel.

Serve with a lemon wedge if desired.

#34: Skillet Cod with Fresh Tomatoes & Basil

Serves: 4

Cook time: 15 minutes

Ingredients

2 tablespoons of fresh basil, chopped

2 cloves of garlic, minced

2 tablespoons of balsamic vinegar

½ cup of chicken or vegetable broth

2 cups of cherry tomatoes

1 medium red onion, cut in half, and sliced

1 tablespoon of olive oil

¼ teaspoon of dried Italian seasoning

Sea salt and pepper to taste

1½ lbs. of cod cut into 4 pieces

Instructions

Season the fish with sea salt, black pepper, and Italian seasoning, then set aside.

Heat the olive oil in a skillet over medium heat and add in the onions until softened, cooking for about 2-3minutes.

Add in the cherry tomatoes, minced garlic, chicken broth, balsamic vinegar, and a tablespoon of basil and cook over medium heat until the tomatoes start to burst — for 4-5 minutes.

Add the fish to the skillet, cook covered for 5 minutes, taste and adjust the seasoning.

Garnish with the remaining tablespoon of basil and enjoy.

#35: Instant Pot Kale, Squash, and Chicken Soup

Serves: 12

Cook time: 30 minutes

Ingredients

Juice of a small lemon

Salt and pepper to taste

6 large kale leaves destemmed and roughly chopped

3 cups of shredded chicken

3 quarts chicken bone broth

1 small butternut squash, peeled and diced

18 oz jar of diced tomatoes

2 tablespoons of Italian seasoning

5 large cloves of garlic, minced

1 yellow onion, diced

2 tablespoons of avocado oil

Instructions

Press Sauté on the instant pot and melt the cooking oil.

Add in the onions and sauté until translucent, then add in the garlic, Italian seasoning, sauté for 1 minute.

Add in the diced tomatoes, squash, broth and replace the lid. Set the valve to sealing and reduce the time to 8 minutes.

Allow the pot to release pressure naturally before carefully opening the lid.

Add in the cooked chicken, kales and press sauté, taste and adjust the seasoning.

Stir the meal and serve.

#36: Turkey Cranberry Meatballs with Cranberry Orange Sauce

Serves: 30 meatballs

Cook time: 30 minutes

Ingredients

½ teaspoon of orange zest

Salt and pepper to taste

1/3 cup almond flour

1 tablespoon of fresh parsley, chopped

1 teaspoon of dried sage

½ cup of shredded apple

1 egg

1 pound of ground turkey

1 large shallot finely diced

2 cloves of garlic, minced

2 teaspoons of olive oil

1 cup of fresh cranberries

Cranberry & orange sauce

½ tablespoon of maple syrup

½ cup of orange juice

1 cup of fresh or frozen cranberries

Instructions

Preheat the oven to 350 degrees F.

Prepare a baking sheet by lining it with parchment paper, then evenly spread a cup of cranberries on the sheet, drizzling on a tablespoon of olive oil.

Place in the oven and bake for 20 minutes until the cranberries are shriveled.

Place a skillet over medium heat, add a teaspoon of olive oil, add the garlic, shallot, and sauté until the shallot softens for 8-10 minutes.

Combine the remaining meatballs ingredients and sauteed shallot and garlic in a bowl until blended.

Add in the oven-baked cranberries and give them a gentle stir.

Make 20 small meatballs, place them on the lined baking tray, and bake until cooked through —for 18 minutes.

Cook the cranberries, orange juice, and maple syrup in a pot over medium heat until the cranberries start popping.

Transfer the cranberries mixture to a blender and blend into a smooth sauce.

Serve the meatballs garnished with parsley and with the cranberry sauce as a dip.

#37: Salmon Balls

Serves: 2-3

Cook time: 30 minutes

Ingredients

1 tablespoon of olive oil

Sea salt and pepper to taste

1 tablespoon of fresh basil, chopped

½ lemon, zested and juiced

1 egg

¼ cup of red onion, finely diced

12 ounces canned wild-caught salmon

Instructions

Preheat the oven to 35 degrees F.

Combine all the ingredients in a bowl, apart from the oil, until well blended.

Make 20 balls.

Prepare a baking tray by spreading some oil on it, then roll the balls in the oil to coat them well.

Place in the oven and bake for 20 minutes.

Serve with a dipping of choice.

#38: Cajun Sweet Potato Fries

Serves: 8

Cook time: 40 minutes

Ingredients

¼ teaspoon of ground cumin

½ teaspoon of oregano

½ teaspoon of cayenne pepper

½ teaspoon of garlic powder

1 teaspoon of onion powder

1¼ teaspoon of smoked paprika

1½ teaspoon of sea salt

2 tablespoons of olive oil

2 pounds of sweet potatoes

Instructions

Preheat the oven to 450 degrees F.

Mix all the ingredients in a large bowl, tossing to coat the sweet potatoes with the spices.

Evenly layer the sweet potatoes on two baking sheets, making sure to avoid overcrowding.

Place the trays in the oven and bake until the sweet potatoes are golden brown —for about 20 minutes.

Use a wide spatula to turn the sweet potato fries.

Broil on high for 5 minutes to desired crispness.

Transfer the lower baking to the top and vice versa, and broil for 3 more minutes.

Serve with your dip of choice.

#39: Slow Cooker Curry Chicken Legs

Serves: 6

Cook time: 4 hours 10 minutes

Ingredients

1 tablespoon of turmeric

1 tablespoon of curry powder

1 teaspoon of salt

1/3 of cup onion optional

½ of cup sweet potatoes

½ of cup carrots

14 ounce can full-fat coconut milk

1 pound of chicken legs

Instructions

Add the milk into the slow cooker and stir in the seasonings.

Place the chicken into the sauce and toss to coat the chicken.

Add in the vegetables, replace the lid, and cook on high heat for 4 hours or on low for 5-6 hours.

Serve warm and enjoy!

#40: Sheet Pan Roasted Brussel sprouts, Butternut, and Bacon

Serves: 6

Cook time: 45 minutes

Ingredients

1 teaspoon of thyme

Salt and pepper to taste

2 teaspoons of gluten-free Dijon mustard

1 tablespoon of balsamic vinegar

3 tablespoons of olive oil

2/3 cup of chopped bacon/pancetta

2 red onions thinly sliced

2 cups of small Brussel sprouts

2 cups cubed butternut squash (approximately 1- inch cubes)

Instructions

Preheat the oven to 400 degrees F.

Wash the Brussel sprouts, cut any tough outer leaves, and cut the larger sprouts in half.

Transfer the cubed butternut, Brussel sprouts, chopped pancetta or bacon, and the red onion onto a large baking sheet.

Whisk the olive oil, balsamic vinegar, Dijon mustard, thyme, salt, and pepper in a bowl, then pour over the vegetables on the baking sheet.

Place the baking sheet in the oven and bake for 35 minutes; toss the veggies halfway through to ensure the veggies cook evenly.

#41: Pan-seared Duck Breast with Cranberry Maple Syrup

Serves: 4

Cook time: 20 minutes

Ingredients

Salt and ground black pepper to taste

1 pound of boneless duck breasts

FOR THE CRANBERRY MAPLE SAUCE

1 sprig of fresh rosemary, leaves removed from stem and minced

Salt to taste

1 tablespoon of maple syrup

1 tablespoon of orange juice

1 teaspoon orange zest

1 cup fresh or frozen cranberries

Instructions

Heat a large cast-iron skillet over medium-high heat.

Score the breast with a sharp knife, make a diagonal diamond pattern, and season with salt and pepper.

Place the duck on the hot skillet, the fat side down.

Sear for about 3-5 minutes until the fat is crispy and turns a deep golden brown.

Flip and sear the other side for an extra 3-5 minutes.

Transfer the duck onto a chopping board, cover, and let it sit for 5-10 minutes before cutting.

Place a small saucepot over medium-low heat, mix all the cranberry sauce ingredients, bring to a simmer, then lower the heat.

Break down the cranberries using a spatula, cooking for about 10 minutes.

Remove from heat and allow to cool.

Serve the duck with the cooled cranberry sauce.

#42: Oven Roasted Brussels Sprouts with Bacon

Serves: 8

Cook time: 30 minutes

Ingredients

10 slices of bacon, cut into ½ inch pieces

Salt and pepper to taste

6 tablespoons of extra-virgin olive oil

2 pounds of brussels sprouts, washed and prepared

Instructions

Preheat the oven to 400 degrees.

Prepare the baking sheet by spraying with cooking spray and put it aside.

Halve the brussels sprouts and place them in a large bowl.

Whisk the oil, salt, pepper in a small bowl until blended.

Drizzle the mixed oil over the brussels sprouts and toss for the oil to coat the sprouts evenly.

Layer the brussels sprouts, with the halved side down, on the prepared baking sheet.

Place the bacon between the sprouts, allowing the bacon to lay on the sheet directly.

Place in the oven, bake for 10 minutes, then flip them over and bake until the sprouts are golden and caramelized —an additional 10 minutes should do it.

Serve and enjoy!

#43: Strawberry Mango Spinach Salad

Serves: 4-6

Cook time: 20 minutes

Ingredients

¼ cup of freshly squeezed lemon juice

1 avocado, pitted, peeled, and diced

2 Champagne mangos

1 pound of strawberries, hulled and sliced

8 ounces of baby spinach, washed

Creamy Basil Dressing:

1 tablespoon of raw, shelled hemp seeds

½ cup of avocado oil

1 teaspoon of gluten-free Dijon mustard

½ teaspoon of sea salt

1 cup of lightly packed basil leaves

Instructions

Place the washed baby spinach in a large serving bowl.

Peel the mangos, cut into half-inch cubes, and add them to the bowl with the spinach.

Add the strawberries and avocado into the bowl with spinach.

Add all the dressing ingredients to the blender and blend until the dressing is creamy.

Stream the dressing over the salad and toss until well mixed.

Serve.

#44: Gluten-Free Chicken Nuggets

Serves: 4

Cook time: 27 minutes

Ingredients

¼ cup of avocado oil

1/8 teaspoon of black pepper

1/8 teaspoon of cayenne pepper

1 teaspoon of paprika

1 teaspoon of garlic powder

¾ teaspoon of salt

¼ cup of almond flour

1lb. of skinless and boneless chicken breast

Instructions

Preheat the oven to 425 degrees for convection or 450 degrees for a conventional oven.

Cut the chicken breasts into 1-inch chunks and transfer them into a bowl.

Combine the flour with the seasonings and coat the chicken chunks with it.

Drizzle melted oil over the chicken and combine to coat lightly.

Place in the oven and bake for 10 minutes.

Serve with a dipping of choice.

#45: Ground Beef with Kale and Mushrooms

Serves: 4

Cook time: 20 minutes

Ingredients

1 pound of ground beef

1 pound bag of frozen chopped kale

10 ounce or larger bag of frozen sliced mushrooms

1½ teaspoon of sea salt

Freshly ground black pepper

½ teaspoon of onion powder

½ teaspoon of garlic powder

½ teaspoon of cayenne pepper

½ teaspoon of crushed red pepper flakes

Instructions

Heat a large skillet over medium heat and add the ground beef. Break the meat up into little pieces with a large spoon or rubber scraper, stirring, then cook until the meat is no longer pink.

Drain the excess liquid and fat from the pan and return it to the heat.

Add the frozen kale, mushrooms, and all of the spices to the cooked ground beef. Stir to combine.

Continue cooking for about five minutes or until the vegetables are warmed through.

Enjoy!

#46: Quiche with Easy Quinoa Crust

Serves: 6

Cook time: 25 minutes

Ingredients

CRUST:

2 teaspoons of dried oregano

Salt and pepper to taste

1 teaspoon of dried basil

1 tablespoon of extra virgin olive oil

2 tablespoons of quinoa or buckwheat

1 egg, beaten

2 cups of cooked quinoa

Filling:

5 eggs

¼ white onion, diced

1/3 cup of sun-dried tomatoes, finely chopped

¼ cup of hemp milk

¼ teaspoon of salt

1 red bell pepper, finely chopped

2 cups of broccoli, cut into small pieces

Instructions

Preheat the oven to 375 degrees and grease a 9-inch pie plate.

Combine all the ingredients for the crust in a bowl, then transfer into the pie plate and press the crust.

Place in the oven and bake for 12-15 minutes

Sauté the broccoli, bell peppers, and onions in a frying pan to a crunchiness of your liking, then transfer the vegetables onto the plate with the crust.

Whisk the eggs, milk, and salt in a small bowl, then pour over the vegetables.

Bake for 25-30 minutes until the eggs quiche cooks through.

#47: Garlic Balsamic Roasted Potatoes and Asparagus

Serves: 4

Cook time: 40 minutes

Ingredients

½ a teaspoon of black pepper, divided

1 teaspoon of kosher salt, divided

1 teaspoon of garlic powder, divided

2 tablespoons of balsamic vinegar, divided

3 tablespoons of avocado oil, divided

1 pound of asparagus spears, ends trimmed and cut into 2" lengths

1½ pounds of small red-skinned potatoes, halved

Instructions

Preheat the oven to 400 degrees F and grease the baking sheet with cooking spray.

Combine the halved potatoes with 2 tablespoons of avocado oil, half the balsamic vinegar, garlic powder, salt, pepper in a large bowl, and toss until well blended.

Spread the potatoes on the prepared baking sheet and roast for 20 minutes, ensuring to toss halfway through.

Add the asparagus, the remaining oil, vinegar, and the rest of the seasonings to the same bowl and toss.

Remove the sheet with the potatoes from the oven, transfer the asparagus into the sheet, and roast in the oven for 10 minutes.

Transfer onto a platter and serve while hot.

#48: Thai Basil Chicken Stir Fry

Serves: 4

Cook time: 20 minutes

Ingredients

4-6 boneless, skinless chicken thighs, cut into 1/2" pieces

1 Thai chili, thinly sliced

2 cloves of garlic, minced

1 cup diced red onion

1 tablespoon of avocado oil

Sauce:

½ a cup of Thai basil leaves

2 tablespoons of fish sauce

¼ cup of gluten-free soy sauce

Instructions

Prepare all the ingredients.

Heat a large skillet over high heat and add the avocado oil, onions, garlic, the chilis, and stir-fry until fragrant —for 2-3 minutes.

Add the chicken and stir-fry until browned —for 2-3 minutes— then pour in the soy and fish sauce and constantly stir for 1-2 minutes.

Turn off the heat, add in the basil leaves and stir.

Serve with sides of choice.

Section 3

Dinner Recipes

#49: Butter bean, chorizo & spinach baked eggs

Serves: 2

Cook time: 20 minutes

Ingredients

4 medium eggs

100g of spinach

400g can of drained gluten-free butter beans

100g chorizo, cut into rounds

1 teaspoon of chili flakes

1 garlic clove, chopped

1 red onion, sliced

½ tablespoon of olive oil

Instructions

Preheat the oven to 220 degrees C.

Place a medium-sized ovenproof frying pan over medium heat, heat your oil, then add in the onions before cooking it about 3 minutes or until the onions start to soften.

Add the garlic, chili flakes, the chorizo, and fry for 2 minutes. Add in the butter beans, then season with a generous pinch of salt.

Stir to combine well and cook for 2 more minutes.

Add the spinach, some water, and whisk until the spinach wilts and set away from heat.

Using the back of a tablespoon, make four dips into the mixture, then crack each egg into the 4 holes.

Season with salt and freshly ground pepper, and add extra chili if desired.

Transfer into the oven and bake for 5-6 minutes until the egg whites set and the yolk runny.

Serve garnished with coriander.

#50: Oven-baked Thai Chicken Rice

Serves: 4

Cook time: 35 minutes

Ingredients

400g of reduced-fat coconut milk

Juice of 1 lime

Finely grated lime zest

2 deseeded red peppers cut into wedges

250g of basmati and wild rice mix, rinsed

400g mini chicken fillet

1 onion chopped

1 tablespoon of vegetable oil

Instructions

Preheat the oven to 200 degrees C.

Add the oil to a shallow ovenproof casserole dish and fry the onions until soft —for 5 minutes.

Add the chicken and the curry paste and cook for 3 minutes, occasionally stirring to coat the chicken with the paste and onions.

Add the rice and peppers to the dish, stir in the lime zest, lime juice, coconut milk, and 250 ml of boiling water.

Bring to a boil, remove the lid, put the dish in the oven, and bake until the rice is fluffy —for about 20 minutes.

Serve garnished with coriander.

#51: Salmon and Avocado Salsa

Serves: 4-6

Cook time: 25 minutes

Ingredients

1-2 tablespoons of olive oil

Sea salt and pepper to taste

1 teaspoon of onion powder

1 teaspoon of smoked paprika

1 teaspoon of cumin

2 pounds of salmon

For the avocado salsa:

Salt and pepper to taste

2 tablespoons of fresh cilantro, chopped

2 tablespoons of olive oil

Juice from 3 limes

3 mild peppers, seeded and finely diced

1 small onion, finely diced

2 avocados, peeled and diced

Instructions

Whisk all the salsa ingredients in a bowl until well mixed.

Transfer the salsa to the fridge.

Preheat the oven to 400 degrees F.

Grease a baking pan/tray and place the salmon on it.

Mix the spices in a small bowl, then coat the salmon with the spices.

Drizzle some olive oil over the salmon and bake in the oven until the salmon cooks through and flakes easily using a fork —for 12-15 minutes.

Serve accompanied with the avocado salsa.

#52: Broccoli & Beef Teriyaki Noodle Bowls

Serves: 4

Cook time: 50 minutes

Ingredients

¼ teaspoon of red pepper flakes

1¼ teaspoons of dried ginger

¼ cup of tamari sauce

¾ cup of gluten-free teriyaki sauce

3 cups of broccoli florets

1.5 pounds of skirt steak sliced thin against the grain

1 onion thinly sliced

4 ounces of thin rice noodles rice sticks

Instructions

Soak the rice noodles for 45 minutes in very hot water as you prepare the beef.

Sauté the onions as well as the beef in a large skillet over medium heat and cook stirring as often as possible.

Whisk the teriyaki sauce, tamari sauce, ginger, and red pepper flakes in a small bowl until mixed well.

Pour the sauce into the skillet with beef and stir, then add the broccoli.

Place the soaked rice noodles in the microwave for 2-3 minutes, then drain.

Transfer the noodles into the skillet with broccoli, beef, sauce and give it a good stir.

Serve and enjoy.

#53: Lemon Chicken and Asparagus Sheet Pan Dinner

Serves: 4-6

Cook time: 45 minutes

Ingredients

1 lemon, cut into thin slices

1 bunch of asparagus, washed and woody stems removed

Sea salt and freshly ground black pepper to taste

¼ cup of freshly squeezed lemon juice

1 tablespoon of lemon zest

1 tablespoon of maple syrup

2 tablespoons of olive oil

1 garlic clove, minced

2 teaspoons of Herbs de Provence

4 chicken breasts, boneless and skinless, about 2 pounds

Instructions

Preheat your oven to 400 degrees F and line a baking tray with parchment paper.

Arrange the chicken breasts evenly on the prepared tray and put them aside.

Whisk the Herb de Provence, minced garlic, olive oil, maple syrup, lemon zest, lemon juice, salt, and pepper in a small bowl until mixed.

Drizzle half of the mixture over the chicken breasts.

Place the baking tray with the chicken breasts in the oven and bake for 20 minutes until the chicken is almost done.

Remove the chicken breasts from the oven and set the oven to broil.

Toss the rest of the mixture with the asparagus and place them around the edges of the tray with the chicken breasts.

Place some lemon wedges or slices around the breasts and the asparagus.

Place the tray in the oven and broil for 10 minutes until the asparagus is crisp.

Serve and enjoy.

#54: Foil Packet Grilled Mahi Mahi

Serves: 2

Cook time: 20 minutes

Ingredients

1 teaspoon of Zaitarin's Cajun Seasoning

Salt to taste

1 lime

1 cup of chopped potatoes

1 pound of asparagus

1 tablespoon of olive oil

4 pieces Open Natur Mahi Mahi, thawed

Instructions

Place the cut potatoes in the microwave for 5 minutes to soften.

Preheat your grill to 375 degrees.

Place the Mahi Mahi fillets on a piece of foil —each.

Place some potatoes and asparagus on each foil with each fish.

Season the fish, potatoes, and asparagus with salt and pepper, then top with lime slices.

Drizzle some olive oil over each packet, fold up and place them on the grill.

Grill for 10 minutes until the potatoes are soft and the fish is firm.

Remove from the foil packets and enjoy.

#55: Roasted Cauliflower & Garlic Soup

Serves: 4

Cook time: 30 minutes

Ingredients

5 cups of chicken or vegetable stock

Salt and pepper to taste

½ teaspoon of smoked paprika

1½ tablespoon of lemon juice

2 tablespoons of olive oil

1 head of garlic

1 large cauliflower

Leeks

Optional Garnish

Truffle oil

¼ cup of cooked pancetta, diced or pumpkin seeds

Instructions

Preheat the oven to 200 degrees C.

Chop the cauliflower into medium-sized pieces, leeks into 2-inch slices, and a 1/3 of the garlic's top, exposing the cloves, then transfer them on a baking sheet.

Season the vegetables with salt and drizzle on some olive oil.

Place in the oven and bake until brown and tender —for about 20 minutes— ensuring to turn the vegetables halfway through baking.

Transfer all the cooked vegetables, lemon juice, smoked paprika, and the 2 cups of chicken or vegetable stock to a blender and blend until smooth.

Place a skillet over medium-low heat, pour in the blended soup and the rest of the stock, and season with salt and pepper.

Ladle the soup in a bowl and garnish with pancetta, pumpkin seeds and drizzle on some truffle oil —if desired.

#56: Instant Pot Ribs

Serves: 6

Cook time: 50 minutes

Ingredients

1 cup of water

3 pounds of sustainably raised spareribs

Dry Rub

1 teaspoon of red pepper flakes

2 teaspoons of paprika

1 tablespoon of sea salt

1 tablespoon of dried parsley

1 tablespoon of garlic powder

Instructions

Combine all the dry rub seasonings.

Dry out all the sides of the ribs and generously season with the dry rub.

Put the trivet in place at the bottom of the pressure cooker, then add a cup of water.

Place the ribs in the pot and secure the lid; adjust the cooking time to 30 minutes.

Allow the pressure cooker to release the pressure naturally for 15 minutes, then do a quick pressure release

Use tongs to transfer the ribs on a lined baking sheet and broil for 4 minutes on high until the ribs are crisp.

Enjoy.

#57: Guacamole Stuffed Chicken Breast

Serves: 4

Cook time: 1 hour

Ingredients

Cooking spray

Salt and pepper to taste

¼ teaspoon of ground cumin

¼ teaspoon of chili powder

½ teaspoon of garlic powder

2 teaspoon of lime zest

1 cup of Gluten-free plain panko breadcrumbs

2 large eggs

¾ teaspoon of salt, divided

1 teaspoon of lime juice

¼ cup of chopped tomato

2 tablespoons of red onion, diced

1 ripe avocado

4 small boneless skinless chicken breasts

Instructions

Preheat the oven to 400 degrees F.

Pound the chicken breast using a mallet until it's thin and flat, then put it aside.

Peel and deseed the avocado and mash using a fork in a medium-sized bowl.

Add the onion, tomato, lime juice, and a ½ teaspoon of salt and whisk until well blended.

Spread a thin layer of the guacamole in the chicken pieces, then roll up the chicken, securing them with toothpicks.

Whisk the eggs in a shallow bowl.

Add pepper, ¼ teaspoon of salt, cumin, chili powder, garlic powder, lime zest, and the breadcrumbs in a bowl and stir to combine.

Roll the chicken in the eggs, allowing any excess egg drip, press and roll the chicken into the bowl with breadcrumbs, shaking off the excess breadcrumbs.

Transfer the coated chicken to a baking dish sprayed with cooking spray and bake in the oven for 30 minutes until the chicken has cooked through.

#58: Ground Turkey Brussels Sprouts Skillet

Serves: 4

Cook time: 30 minutes

Ingredients

½ pound of brussels sprouts, shredded

1 bell pepper, diced

½ teaspoon of cayenne

½ teaspoon of black pepper

Salt to taste

2 teaspoons of chili powder

4 cloves of garlic, minced

1 pound of ground turkey

1 onion, diced

3 tablespoons of coconut oil, divided

Instructions

Place a large skillet over medium heat and melt two tablespoons of coconut oil.

Add in the onions and fry until soft —for 5 minutes.

Add the ground turkey, garlic, and the other spices, then cook until the meat completely cooks through —for 15-20 minutes.

Spoon some meat in a bowl, making room for the Brussel sprouts.

Melt the rest of the coconut oil in the skillet, then add in the brussels sprouts and the bell pepper and stir-fry until tender.

Transfer the meat back in the skillet stir until well mixed.

Serve and enjoy!

#59: Spicy Shrimp and Brussels Sprout Stir-Fry

Serves: 4

Cook time: 20 minutes

Ingredients

Lime wedges, for serving

2 teaspoons of toasted sesame oil

1 pound of medium shrimp, peeled, deveined, and tails left on

3 scallions, with the white and green parts separated and thinly sliced

1 small green Thai chili, thinly sliced

2 cloves of garlic, thinly sliced

1 cup of bean sprouts

Salt and pepper to taste

1 pound brussels sprouts, trimmed and shredded

2 tablespoons vegetable oil, divided

Instructions

Place a wok over medium-high heat and heat a tablespoon of the vegetable oil.

Sauté the brussels sprouts in two batches for 5 minutes in total until tender and season with salt and pepper to taste.

Add in the bean sprouts and cook for 1 minute, then transfer onto a platter.

Wipe the pan clean, then add the other tablespoon of vegetable oil.

Then proceed to add the scallion whites, chili and the garlic then cook for 30 seconds until fragrant.

Add in the shrimp, season with salt and pepper, and sauté for 4 minutes until opaque, then transfer to the platter and drizzle with sesame oil, topped with scallion greens, then toss.

Serve with lemon wedges if desired

#60: Ground Beef Curry

Serves: 4

Cook time: 45 minutes

Ingredients

3 cups of peas

3 medium potatoes

3 cups of tomatoes

1/8 teaspoon of turmeric

1/8 teaspoon of ginger

1/8 teaspoon of cinnamon

1/8 teaspoon of pepper

Salt to taste

1½ tablespoons of curry powder

1lb. of ground beef

1 cup of chopped onion

2-3 tablespoons of coconut oil

Instructions

Melt the coconut oil in a large pan.

Add in the onion, garlic and cook until the onions are soft — be sure not to burn the garlic.

Add the minced meat and allow it to cook through, then add in the curry, salt, and the spices, then stir to combine.

Dice the potatoes before adding them to the pan, add in the tomatoes and bring to simmer.

Lower the heat and cook covered until the potatoes are done —for 10-15 minutes.

Add the peas and cook until they are done.

Serve as desired.

#61: Maple Mustard Chicken with Fall Vegetables

Serves: 4

Cook time: 30 minutes

Ingredients

Salt and pepper to taste

½ a tablespoon of minced fresh rosemary plus more for roasting

1 tablespoon of apple cider vinegar

1 tablespoon of maple syrup

1 tablespoon of minced garlic

2 tablespoons of gluten-free Dijon mustard

½ cup of fresh or frozen cranberries

1 pound of delicata squash, sliced into rings and seeds removed

12 ounces of brussels sprouts, trimmed and halved

1¼ pounds of chicken breast

Instructions

Preheat your oven to 40 degrees F and grease a large baking sheet with cooking spray.

Lay the chicken breasts on the prepared baking sheet and season with salt and pepper.

Scatter the squash, sprouts, and cranberries around the chicken.

Whip the mustard, garlic, maple syrup, apple cider vinegar, minced rosemary, and the salt and pepper in a small bowl and spoon over each chicken breast, then drizzle the rest of the sauce over the vegetables.

Place in the preheated oven and bake for 18-20 minutes until the chicken cooks through.

Let the meal sit for 5 minutes before slicing and serving the chicken.

#62: Instant Pot Spicy Orange Beef

Serves: 4

Cook time: 25 minutes

Ingredients

1 bunch of green onions, chopped

3 tablespoons of cold water

2 tablespoons of arrowroot powder

1 teaspoon of orange zest

½ teaspoon of crushed red pepper flakes

2 teaspoons of sesame oil

¼ cup of coconut aminos or organic tamari

¾ cup of orange juice

1 tablespoon of avocado oil

2 lbs. of flank steak, cut into ¼ strips

2 bell peppers, your color of choice

6 cloves of garlic, minced

Instructions

Deseed and destem the bell peppers, then cut into strips and put aside.

Season the steak strips with salt and pepper.

Add oil to the instant pot, select the sauté function, brown the meat in batches, then transfer to a plate.

Add garlic to the pot and cook for a minute.

Add the orange juice, soy sauce, sesame oil, red pepper flakes, orange zest, and browned beef to the instant pot.

Select the high-pressure function on the pot and set it for 12 minutes.

Turn the pot off, do a quick pressure release, then remove the lid carefully.

Add the striped bell peppers to the pot.

Whisk the arrowroot powder with the water until smooth, then add the mixture to the pot and stir constantly.

Select the sauté function and allow to boil, constantly stirring until the sauce thickens.

Add in the green onions and stir.

Serve garnished with orange zest, green onions, or red pepper flakes if desired.

#63: Turkey Sweet Potato Skillet

Serves: 4

Cook time: 30 minutes

Ingredients

Avocado slices for serving

Lime wedges for serving

Salt and pepper to taste

½ teaspoon of smoked paprika

½ teaspoon of cumin

1 teaspoon of garlic powder

2 cups of baby greens

1 yellow bell pepper, chopped

15 ounce can of black beans, drained and rinsed

1 cup of shredded turkey

1/3 cup of vegetable or chicken broth

1 large sweet potato, peeled and chopped into cubes

1 medium yellow onion, chopped

1 tablespoon avocado oil

Instructions

Heat the avocado oil in a large skillet over medium heat.

Add the onions and sweet potatoes and stir until combined.

Cook until the onions are soft, for about 2-3 minutes.

Add the chicken or vegetable broth to the skillet, cover, and bring to simmer for 8-10 minutes on medium-low heat, until sweet potatoes are tender.

Add the black beans, peppers, and the baby greens, stir and cook until the peppers soften, for about 3-5 minutes.

Adjust seasoning by adding the spices, salt, and pepper to taste.

Serve garnished with lime wedges and avocado.

#64: Red Rice with Sausage and Peppers

Serves: 4

Cook time: 25 minutes

Ingredients

2 cups of Simple White Rice

1 can of diced tomatoes

Coarse salt and ground pepper to taste

1 celery stalk, diced medium

1 red bell pepper, diced medium

2 garlic cloves, minced

1 medium yellow onion, diced medium

12 ounces smoked sausage, cut into small pieces

1 tablespoon extra-virgin olive oil

Instructions

Heat oil in a skillet over medium-high heat, add in the sausage and cook, occasionally stirring for bout 8 minutes until crispy.

Add the onions, garlic, red pepper, celery, salt, and pepper and cook stirring until the celery softens —for 8 minutes.

Add the tomatoes and cook for 3 minutes until they thicken slightly.

Add the rice and cook for 2 minutes until warmed through.

#65: Red Curry Chicken Wings

Serves: 4

Cook time: 4 hours 10 minutes

Ingredients

2 tablespoons of cold water

¼ cup of fresh basil, finely shredded, for serving

Limes for serving

2 tablespoons of arrowroot powder

3 lbs. of chicken wings

3 tablespoons of red curry paste

1 tablespoon of fish sauce

1 cup of coconut milk

Instructions

Mix the coconut milk, fish sauce, and curry paste in a bowl.

Add the wings to a slow cooker and pour the sauce over them.

Replace the lid and cook covered on low for 4 hours.

Remove the chicken from the cooker using a slotted spoon and put it aside.

Preheat the broiler.

Whisk the arrowroot and water to make a slurry.

Add the remaining sauce to a medium saucepan, then add the slurry to the sauce. Bring to a boil, then let simmer until the sauce thickens for about 10-15 minutes.

Toss the wings in the thickened sauce, then layer the pieces on the broiler pan.

Broil the chicken until browned 4-5 inches away from the heat and turn once.

Garnish with shredded basil and fresh limes.

#66: Instant Pot Venison Roast

Serves: 6

Cook time: 1 hour 40 minutes

Ingredients

8 ounces cremini mushrooms, halved

1 medium red onion, roughly chopped

½ pound of carrots, roughly chopped into 1 to 1.5" pieces

1½ pounds of baby potatoes, scrubbed but left whole

5 sprigs of fresh thyme

3 sprigs of fresh rosemary

2 tablespoons of balsamic vinegar

½ cup of beef broth

1 cup of red wine

Salt and pepper to taste

2 pounds of venison roast

1 tablespoon of avocado oil

Instructions

Place the avocado oil in the insert of the instant pot and turn it to sauté mode.

Generously season the venison roast with salt and pepper on all the sides.

Transfer the seasoned roast to the pot and brown all sides.

Turn off the instant pot, pour in the red wine, broth, vinegar, and add the herbs.

Replace the lid, set the valve to sealing, and cook on stew mode for 70 minutes.

Do a quick pressure release, open the lid, add in the potatoes, carrots, onions, and mushrooms.

Replace the lid, set the valve to sealing, and manual mode for 12 minutes.

Do another quick pressure release, then transfer the venison on a chopping board and let it sit for 5-10 minutes before slicing.

Transfer the sliced venison on a serving platter, then scatter the veggies around.

Spoon out any sauce left in the instant pot in a small bowl for serving.

#67: Baked Chicken Thighs

Serves: 6

Cook time: 30 minutes

Ingredients

Salt and pepper to taste

½ a teaspoon of garlic powder

1 lemon, sliced into rounds

3-5 sprigs of fresh rosemary

3-5 sprigs of fresh thyme

6 large, bone-in chicken thighs

2 tablespoons of olive oil

Instructions

Preheat oven to 450 degrees F. Place a cast-iron skillet over medium-high heat and pour in the olive oil.

Dry out the chicken thighs with paper towels. Season the thighs with garlic powder, salt, and pepper.

Place the thighs in the skillet with the skin side down and sear until the skin is golden brown —for about 5-7 minutes.

Turn the chicken thighs and add in the fresh herbs and the lemon slices.

Turn off the heat, transfer the skillet to the oven, and roast the chicken thighs for 15-18 minutes.

Serve and enjoy warm.

#68: Quinoa Stuffed Chicken

Serves: 4

Cook time: 50 minutes

Ingredients

1 teaspoon of salt

1 teaspoon of chili powder

1 teaspoon of ground cumin

1 lime, zest, and 1 tablespoon of the juice

¼ cup of chopped cilantro

1/3 cup of shaved coconut (unsweetened) (coconut chips)

1 serrano pepper, seeded and diced

2 cloves of garlic, minced

½ cup of red onion, diced

¾ cup of red and yellow bell peppers, diced

1 tablespoon of coconut oil

1½ cups of chicken broth

¾ cups quinoa, any color

4 boneless chicken breasts, skinless

Instructions

Start by preheating your oven to 375 degrees F then start preparing a rimmed baking sheet on the side by using a parchment paper to line it.

Heat a medium saucepan over medium-high heat and melt the coconut oil, then add in the bell peppers, red onion, garlic, the serrano pepper, and sauté for 1-2 minutes.

Transfer the veggies to a bowl.

Add the quinoa to the now-empty pot, adjust the heat from medium to high, then pour in the chicken broth and season with ½ a teaspoon of salt.

Replace the lid, bring it to a boil, then let it cook for 15 minutes until all the broth has been absorbed. Set the pot off the heat and allow the quinoa to steam for 5 minutes.

Slit the chicken breasts along one long side using a boning knife, cutting through the center, making sure the opposite side is intact, creating a deep pocket in each breast.

Season the slit chicken breasts with cumin, chili powder, and salt.

Stir in the sauteed vegetables, lime juice, lime zest, cilantro, and the shaved coconut, into the now fluffy quinoa, then proceed to taste, and adjust seasoning.

Scoop and then stuff the confetti quinoa inside the pockets in each chicken breast.

Transfer the stuffed chicken breasts on the rimmed baking sheet then let them stand like open envelopes. Place the sheet in the oven and bake for 2 minutes.

Serve and enjoy warm.

#69: Keto coconut curry chicken

Serves: 4

Cook time: 50 minutes

Ingredients

1 lime, the finely grated zest

14 oz. of coconut cream

½ red chili pepper, finely chopped

1 red bell pepper, sliced

2 garlic cloves

1 thumb-sized piece of fresh ginger

1 leek

1½ lbs. boneless chicken thighs

1 tablespoon of curry powder

2 tablespoons of coconut oil

2 stalks of lemongrass

Instructions

Cut the chicken into pieces.

Heat a wok over medium heat and add in the coconut oil.

Add in grated ginger, lemongrass, curry, and fry.

Add in half of the chicken and sauté until golden.

Season with salt and pepper.

Transfer onto a platter, leaving the lemongrass in the wok, and set aside.

Sauté sliced leeks in the wok with the rest of the vegetables and garlic until golden.

Add in the rest of the uncooked chicken and fry chicken as the first batch.

Add in the coconut cream and the 1st batch of the chicken that you set aside, allow to simmer for 5-10 minutes until everything warms up.

#70: Shrimp and Scallion Stir-Fry

Serves: 4

Cook time: 15 minutes

Ingredients

Cooked rice for serving

Salt to taste

2tablespoons of fresh lemon juice

2 bunches of scallions, cut into 1 ½ inch pieces

½ teaspoon of red pepper flakes

2 cloves of garlic, minced

1pound of large shrimp, peeled and deveined

1 tablespoon of vegetable oil

Instructions

Place a wok over high heat, add the oil, and swirl to coat the wok.

Add in the shrimp and stir for 1-2 minutes until almost pink.

Stir in the garlic, red pepper flakes, and fry until fragrant — for 30 seconds.

Add in the scallions, stir for about a minute until they're bright green.

Pour in the lemon juice and 2 tablespoons of water and cook for another minute.

Adjust seasoning and serve over rice if desired.

#71: Easy Jambalaya

Serves: 6

Cook time: 55 minutes

Ingredients

Salt and pepper to taste

2 teaspoons of lemon zest

¼ cup of freshly chopped parsley

1 pound of cleaned medium, raw shrimp

2½ cups of chicken broth

1¼ cups of long grain rice

1 tablespoon of fresh thyme leaves

15 ounces of plum tomatoes, canned in juices

2-3 stalks of celery, Sliced

1 large bell pepper, seeded and chopped

1 tablespoon of Tastefully Simple® Garlic Seasoning

1 large sweet onion, peeled and chopped

1 pound of andouille-style chicken sausages, sliced

2 tablespoons of Tastefully Simple® Roasted Garlic Infused Oil

Instructions

Place a large 6-8quart Dutch oven over medium heat, add in the garlic-infused oil and the sliced sausages.

Flip the sausages using a wooden spoon until all sides are brown.

Move the sausage pieces to the sides of the pot, then add the onions and the garlic seasoning in the middle.

Sauté the onions for 5 minutes, occasionally stirring until tender, then stir in the bell pepper and celery, sauté for an extra 1-2 minutes.

Pour the tomato juices into the pot, crush the tomatoes in your hands, transfer into the pot, then stir in the thyme, the rice, chicken broth, ½ a teaspoon of salt, and a ¼ teaspoon of black pepper.

Replace the lid, bring to a boil, then reduce the heat and simmer, give the food a fine stir, cover and simmer undisturbed for 18-20 minutes.

Stir in the shrimp once the rice cooks through and cook until the shrimp turn pink for an additional 2-3 minutes.

Stir in the parsley, the lemon zest, taste, and adjust seasoning.

Serve.

#72: Salmon with olive-pistachio tapenade and tomatoes

Serves: 2

Cook time: 35 minutes

Ingredients

¼ cup of olive oil

Salt and pepper to taste

¼ cup of fresh dill, chopped

½ tablespoon of dried thyme

10 oz. of cherry tomatoes with stems

14 oz. of salmon, boneless fillets

1½ oz. of pistachio nuts, shelled

2 oz. of green olives, pitted

Instructions

Preheat the oven to 180 degrees C.

Finely chop the olives and pistachios, then put them in a small bowl, add in a splash of olive oil, and stir until blended.

Place the salmon fillets in a baking dish and spread the olives mixture all over and between the fillets.

Add the tomatoes to a different baking dish, season with salt, pepper, and thyme, then drizzle on some olive oil.

Place the baking dishes in the oven and bake for 15 minutes until the fillets are opaque at the center.

Garnish the salmon with dill before serving.

#73: Kielbasa and Lentil Rice with Spinach

Serves: 4

Cook time: 1 hour

Ingredients

1 bunch of fresh spinach, thick stems removed, torn into 2-inch pieces

2 tablespoons of apple cider vinegar

15 ounces of crushed tomatoes

½ cup of long-grain white rice

½ cup of green or brown lentils, picked through and rinsed

4 teaspoons of curry powder

Kosher salt and freshly ground pepper to taste

1 medium onion, chopped

1 pound of kielbasa or any other smoked sausage

2 tablespoons of extra-virgin olive oil

Instructions

Place a large straight-sided skillet over medium heat and heat the oil, prick the kielbasa with a fork, then gently place in the skillet.

Fry the kielbasa for 5-7 minutes, flipping until well browned all over, then transfer to a plate.

Add the onions to the skillet, lower the heat, season the onions with salt, and fry, occasionally stirring for 5-6 minutes until the onions are golden.

Add in the curry powder, stir and cook for 30 seconds before adding the lentils and 2½ cups of water, allow to boil, lower the heat, cover and bring to simmer for 10 minutes.

Stir in the rice, tomatoes, vinegar, and season with salt and pepper before transferring the kielbasa and any juices back to the skillet.

Replace the lid and simmer over low heat for 15 minutes until the rice and the lentils cook through.

Add in the spinach, and cook for 2-3 minutes until just wilted, stir, taste, and adjust seasoning.

Serve having sliced the kielbasa.

#74: Prosciutto-Wrapped Salmon Skewers

Serves: 4

Cook time: 25 minutes

Ingredients

1 tablespoon of olive oil

1 cup of mayonnaise for serving

3½ oz. of prosciutto, in thin slices

1 pinch of ground black pepper

1lb. of skinless salmon, boneless fillets, frozen in pieces

¼ cup of fresh basil, finely chopped

Salmon skewers

Instructions

Preheat the oven to 180 degrees C.

Soak skewers in water and thaw the salmon.

Cut the salmon after it thaws into ½ inch wide pieces and stick onto the skewers.

Roll the salmon skewers in the chopped basil and pepper and wrap the salmon with the sliced prosciutto.

Bake the skewers in the oven for 15 minutes, flip the skewers halfway through until the prosciutto is crisp.

Serve with mayonnaise and salad of choice if desired.

Conclusion

As you have seen, following a gluten-free, dairy-free, and sugar-free diet does not have to be restrictive. There's a wide range of easy-to-make and child-friendly recipes to follow, from seafood, vegetables to beef and chicken.

Thank you for reading this guide!

PS: I'd like your feedback. If you are happy with this book, please leave a review on Amazon.

Please leave a review for this book on Amazon by visiting the page below:

https://amzn.to/2VMR5qr

Printed in Poland
by Amazon Fulfillment
Poland Sp. z o.o., Wrocław
29 October 2022

bfd1b964-1772-4cde-8041-a1e8eb3a8ee5R01